Mindfulness is the path to the deathless;
Heedlessness is the path to death.
The mindful do not die;
But the heedless are as if dead already.

Dhammapada 21

จัดพิมพ์เป็นธรรมทานโดย

ฯพณฯ ประจวบ ไชยสาส์น รัฐมนตรีว่าการกระทรวงวิทยาศาสตร์
    เทคโนโลยีและการพลังงาน และคุณทับทิม ไชยสาส์น
พลตำรวจเอก วสิษฐ เดชกุญชร
พลโท มงคล อัมพรพิสิฏฐ์
คุณเสรี ทองวานิช
คุณเลิศ วีระมน
คุณชุมพล รังควร
พันตำรวจเอก ชาตรี - คุณกนก เพชร์คำ
ดร.ทอง ดาวเรือง
คุณวิสาท ภานุทัต
คุณรัชกิจ - คุณพรเพ็ญ บุญรอดพานิช และคณะ

Mindfulness: The Path to the Deathless

The Meditation Teaching of Venerable Ajahn Sumedho

Reprinted and Donated by

The Buddhist Association of the United States

美國佛教會

3070 Albany Crescent,
Bronx, NY 10463
Tel: (718)884-9111

First published in 1985 as *Path to the Deathless*.
This edition re-edited and reset, and published by

Amaravati Publications
Amaravati Buddhist Centre
Great Gaddesden
Hemel Hempstead
Hertfordshire HP1 3BZ
England

ISBN 1 870205 01 4

Contents

Introduction

The aim of this book is to provide a clear instruction in and reflection on Buddhist meditation as taught by Ajahn Sumedho, a bhikkhu (monk) of the Theravadin tradition. The following chapters are edited from longer talks Ajahn Sumedho has given to meditators as a practical approach to the wisdom of Buddhism. This wisdom is otherwise known as Dhamma, or 'the way things are'.

You are invited to use this book as a step-by-step manual. The first chapter tries to make the practice of meditation clear in a general way and the subsequent sections can be taken one at a time and followed by a period of meditation. The third chapter is a reflection on the understanding that meditation develops. The book concludes with the means of taking the Refuges and Precepts which place the practice of meditation within the larger framework of mind-cultivation. These can be requested formally from ordained Buddhists (Saṅgha) or personally determined. They form the foundation of the means whereby spiritual values are brought into the world.

The first edition of this book (2,000 copies) was printed in 1985 – for the opening of the Amaravati Buddhist Centre – and stocks were quickly exhausted. People appreciated the book, and some asked to help sponsor a re-print; so we gave the manuscript a more-thorough proof-reading than had been possible before, and added some design to improve the 'feel' of the book. – otherwise the text is the same. As this book is entirely produced by voluntary contributions and acts of service to the Dhamma, readers are asked to respect this offering and make it freely available.

May all beings realise Truth.

Venerable Sucitto
Amaravati Buddhist Centre
May 1986

A note before you begin

Most of these instructions can be carried out whether sitting, standing or walking. However, the technique of mindfulness of breathing (ānāpānasati) mentioned in the first few chapters is generally used with a sitting posture as it is improved by a still and settled physical state. For this state the emphasis is on sitting in such a way that the spine is erect, but not stressed, with the neck in line with the spine and the head balanced so that it does not droop forward. Many people find the crosslegged 'lotus' posture (sitting on a cushion or mat with one or both feet placed sole upward on the opposite thigh) an ideal balance of effort and stability – after a few months of practice. It is good to train oneself towards this, gently, a little at a time. A straight-backed chair can be used if this posture is too difficult.

Having attained some physical balance and stability, the arms and face should be relaxed, with the hands resting, one in the palm of the other, in the lap. Allow the eyelids to close, relax the mind... take up the meditation object.

'Jongrom' (a Thai word derived from *caṅkama* from Pāli, the scriptural language) means pacing to and fro on a straight path. The path should be measured – ideally twenty to thirty paces – between two clearly recognisable objects, so that one is not having to count the steps. The hands should be lightly clasped in front of or behind the body with the arms relaxed. The gaze should be directed in an unfocussed way on the path about ten paces ahead – not to observe anything, but to maintain the most comfortable angle for the neck. The walking then begins in a composed' manner, and when one reaches the end of the path, one stands still for the period of a breath or two, mindfully turns around, and mindfully walks back again.

10

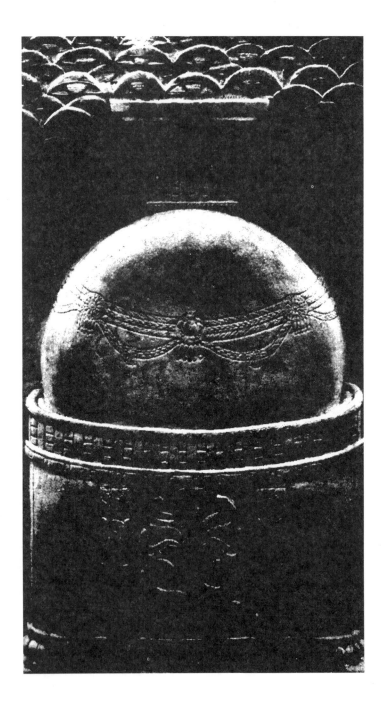

Investigation

What is Meditation?

The word meditation is a much used word these days, covering a wide range of practices. In Buddhism it designates two kinds of meditation – one is called 'samatha', the other 'vipassanā'. Samatha meditation is one of concentrating the mind on an object, rather than letting it wander off to other things. One chooses an object such as the sensation of breathing, and puts full attention on the sensations of the inhalation and exhalation. Eventually through this practice you begin to experience a calm mind – and you become tranquil because you are cutting off all other impingements that come through the senses.

The objects that you use for tranquillity are tranquillising (needless to say!). If you want to have an excited mind, then go to something that is exciting, don't go to a Buddhist monastery, go to a disco! ... Excitement is easy to concentrate on, isn't it? It's so strong a vibration that it just pulls you right into it. You go to the cinema and if it is really an exciting film, you become enthralled by it. You don't have to exert any effort to watch something that is very exciting or romantic or adventurous. But if you are not used to it, watching a tranquillising object can be terribly boring. What is more boring than watching your breath if you are used to more exciting things? So for this kind of ability, you have to arouse effort from your mind, because the breath is not interesting, not romantic, not adventurous or scintillating – it is just as it is. So you have to arouse effort because you're not getting stimulated from outside.

In this meditation, you are not trying to create any image, but just to concentrate on the ordinary feeling of your body as it is right now: to sustain and hold your attention on your breathing. When you do that, the breath becomes more and more refined, and you calm down...I know people who have prescribed samatha meditation for high blood pressure because it calms the heart.

So this is tranquillity practice. You can choose different objects to concentrate on, training yourself to sustain your attention till you absorb or become one with the object. You actually feel a sense of oneness with the object you have been concentrating on, and this is what we call absorption.

The other practice is 'vipassanā', or 'insight meditation.' With insight meditation you are opening the mind up to everything. You are not choosing any particular object to concentrate on or absorb into, but watching in order to understand the way things are. Now what we can see about the way things are, is that all sensory experience is impermanent. Everything you see, hear, smell, taste, touch; all mental conditions – your feelings, memories and thoughts – are changing conditions of the mind, which arise and pass away. In vipassanā, we take this characteristic of impermanence (or change) as a way of looking at all sensory experience that we can observe while sitting here.

This is not just a philosophical attitude or a belief in a particular Buddhist theory: impermanence is to be insightfully known by opening the mind to watch, and being aware of the way things are. It's not a matter of analysing things by assuming that things should be a certain way and, when they aren't, then trying to figure out why things are not the way we think they should be. With insight practice, we are not trying to analyse ourselves or even trying to change anything to fit our desires. In this practice we just patiently observe that whatever arises passes away, whether it is mental or physical.

So this includes the sense organs themselves, the object of the senses, and the consciousness that arises with their contact. There are also mental conditions of liking or disliking what we see, smell, taste, feel or touch; the names we give them; and the ideas, words and concepts we create around sensory experience. Much of our life is based on wrong assumptions made through not understanding and not really investigating the way anything is. So life for one who isn't awake and aware tends to become depressing or bewildering, especially when disappointments or tragedies occur. Then one becomes overwhelmed because one has not observed the way things are.

In Buddhist terms we use the word Dhamma, or Dharma, which means 'the way it is', 'the natural laws'. When we observe and 'practise the Dhamma', we open our mind to the way things are. In this way we are no longer blindly reacting to the sensory experience, but understanding it, and through that comprehension beginning to let go of it. We begin to free ourselves from just being overwhelmed or blinded and deluded by the appearance of things. Now to be aware and awake is not a matter of *becoming* that way, but of *being* that way. So we observe the way it is right now, rather than doing something now to become aware in the future. We observe the body as it is, sitting here. It all belongs to nature, doesn't it? The human body belongs to the earth, it needs to be sustained by the things that come out of the earth. You cannot live on just air or try to import food from Mars and Venus. You have to eat the things that live and grow on this Earth. When the body dies, it goes back to the earth, it rots and decays and becomes one with the earth again. It follows the laws of nature, of creation and destruction, of being born and then dying. Anything that is born doesn't stay permanently in one state, it grows up, gets old and then dies. All things in nature, even the universe itself, have their spans of existence, birth and death, beginning and ending. All that we perceive and can conceive of is change; it is impermanent. So it can never permanently satisfy you.

In Dhamma practice, we also observe this unsatisfactoriness of sensory experience. Now just note in your own life that when you expect to be satisfied from sensory objects or experiences you can only be temporarily satisfied, gratified maybe, momentarily happy – and then it changes. This is because there is no point in sensory consciousness that has a permanent quality or essence. So the sense experience is always a changing one, and out of ignorance and not understanding, we tend to expect a lot from it. We tend to demand, hope and create all kinds of things, only to feel terribly disappointed, despairing, sorrowful and frightened. Those very expectations and hopes take us to despair, anguish, sorrow and grief, lamentation, old age, sickness and death.

Now this is a way of examining sensory consciousness. The mind can think in abstractions, it can create all kinds of ideas and images, it can make things very refined or very coarse. There is a whole gamut of possibilities from very refined states of blissful happiness and ecstasies to very coarse painful miseries: from Heaven to Hell, using more picturesque terminology. But there is no permanent Hell and no permanent Heaven, in fact no permanent state that can be perceived or conceived of. In our meditation, once we begin to realise the limitations, the unsatisfactoriness, the changing nature of all sensory experience, we also begin to realise it is not me or mine, it is 'anattā', not self.

So, realising this, we begin to free ourselves from identification with the sensory conditions. Now this is done not through aversion to them, but through understanding them as they are. It is a truth to be realised, not a belief. 'Anattā' is not a Buddhist belief but an actual realisation. Now if you don't spend any time in your life trying to investigate and understand it, you will probably live your whole life on the assumption that you are your body. Even though you might at some moment think, "Oh, I am not the body", you read some kind of inspired poetry or some new philosophical angle. You might think it is a good idea that one isn't the body, but you haven't really *realised* that. Even though some people, intellectuals and so forth, will say, "We are not the body, the body is not self", that is easy to say, but to really *know* that is something else. Through this practice of meditation, through the investigation and understanding of the way things are, we begin to free ourselves from attachment. When we no longer expect or demand, then of course we don't feel the resulting despair and sorrow and grief when we don't get what we want. So this is the goal – 'Nibbāna', or realisation of non-grasping of any phenomena that have a beginning and an ending. When we let go of this insidious and habitual attachment to what is born and dies, we begin to realise the Deathless.

Some people just live their lives reacting to life because they have been conditioned to do so, like Pavlovian dogs. If you are not awakened to the way things are, then you really are merely a conditioned intelligent creature rather than a conditioned stupid dog. You may look down on Pavlov's dogs that salivate when the bell rings, but notice how we do very similar things. This is because with sensory experience it is all conditioning, it is not a person, it is no 'soul' or 'personal essence'. These bodies, feelings, memories and thoughts are perceptions conditioned into the mind through pain, through having been born as a human being, being born into the families we have, and the class, race, nationality; dependent on whether we have a male or female body, attractive or unattractive, and so forth. All these are just the conditions that are not ours, not me, not mine. These conditions, they follow the laws of nature, the natural laws. We cannot say, "I don't want my body to get old" – well, we can say that, but no matter how insistent we are, the body still gets old. We cannot expect the body to never feel pain or get ill or always have perfect vision and hearing. We hope, don't we? "I hope I will always be healthy, I will never become an invalid and I will always have good eyesight, never become blind; have good ears so I will never be one of those old people that others have to yell at; and that I will never get senile and always have control of my faculties 'til I die at ninety-five, fully alert, bright, cheerful, and die just in my sleep without any pain." That is how we would all like it. Some of us might hold up for a long time and die in an idyllic way, tomorrow all our eyeballs might fall out. It is unlikely, but it could happen! However, the burden of life diminishes considerably when we reflect on the limitations of our life. Then we know what we can achieve, what we can learn from life. So much human misery comes out of expecting a lot and never quite being able to get everything one has hoped for.

So in our meditation and insightful understanding of the way things are, we see that beauty, refinement, pleasure are impermanent conditions – as well as pain, misery and ugliness. If you really understand that, then you can enjoy and endure whatever happens to you. Actually, much of the lesson in life is learning to endure what we don't like in ourselves and in the world around us; being able to be patient and kindly, and not make a scene over the imperfections in the sensory experience. We can adapt and endure and accept the changing characteristics of the sensory birth and death cycle by letting go and no longer attaching to it. When we free ourselves from identity with it, we experience our true nature, which is bright, clear, knowing; but is not a personal thing anymore, it is not 'me' or 'mine' – there is no attainment or attachment to it. We can only attach to that which is not ourself!

The Buddha's teachings are merely helpful means, ways of looking at sensory experience that help us to understand it. They are not commandments, they are not religious dogmas that we have to accept or believe in. They are merely guides to point to the way things are. So we are not using the Buddha's teachings to grasp them as an end in themselves, but only to remind ourselves to be awake, alert and aware that all that arises passes away.

This is a continuous, constant observation and reflection on the sensory world, because the sensory world has a powerfully strong influence. Having a body like this with the society we live in, the pressures on all of us are fantastic. Everything moves so quickly – television and the technology of the age, the cars – everything tends to move at a very fast pace. It is all very attractive, exciting and interesting, and it all pulls your senses out. Just notice when you go to London how all the advertisements pull your attention out to whiskey bottles and cigarettes! Your attention is pulled into things you can buy, always going towards rebirth into sensory experience. The materialistic society tries to arouse greed so you will spend your money, and yet never be contented with what you have. There is always something better, something newer, something more delicious than what was the most delicious yesterday... it goes on and on and on, pulling you out into objects of the senses like that.

But when we come into the shrine room, we are not here to look at each other or to be attracted or pulled into any of the objects in the room, but to use them for reminding ourselves. We are reminded to either concentrate our minds on a peaceful object, or open the mind, investigate and reflect on the way things are. We have to experience this, each one for ourselves. No-one's enlightenment is going to enlighten any of the rest of us. So this is a movement inwards: not looking outwards for somebody who is enlightened to make you enlightened. We give this opportunity for encouragement and guidance so that those of you who are interested in doing this can do so. Here you can, most of the time, be sure that nobody is going to snatch your purse! These days you can't count on anything, but there is less risk of it here than if you were sitting in Piccadilly Circus; Buddhist monasteries are refuges for this kind of opening of the mind. This is our opportunity as human beings.

As a human being we have a mind that can reflect and observe. You can observe whether you are happy or miserable. You can observe the anger or jealousy or confusion in you mind. When you are sitting and feel really confused and upset, there is that in you which knows it. You might hate it and just blindly react to it, but if you are more patient you can observe that this is a temporary changing condition of confusion or anger or greed. But an animal

19

cannot do that; when it is angry it is completely that, lost in it. Tell an angry cat to watch its anger! I have never been able to get anywhere with our cat, she cannot reflect on greed. But *I* can, and I am sure that the rest of you can. I see delicious food in front of me, and the movement in the mind is the same as our cat Doris's. But we can observe the animal attraction to things that smell good and look good.

This is using wisdom by watching that impulse, and understanding it. That which observes greed is not greed: greed cannot observe itself, but that which is not greed can observe it. This observing is what we call 'Buddha' or 'Buddha wisdom' – awareness of the way things are.

Instruction

Watching the Breath (Ānāpānasati)

Ānāpānasati* is a way of concentrating your mind on your breath, so whether you are an expert at it already or whether you have given it up as a lost cause, there is always a time to watch the breath. This is an opportunity for developing 'samādhi' (concentration) through mustering all your attention just on the sensation of breathing. So at this time use your full commitment to that one point for the length of an inhalation, and the length of an exhalation. You are not trying to do it for, say, fifteen minutes, because you would never succeed at that, if that were your designated span of time for one-pointed concentration. So use this span of an inhalation and an exhalation.

Now the success of this depends on your patience rather than on your will-power, because the mind does wander and we always have to patiently go back to the breath. When we're aware that the mind wanders off, we note what it is: it may be because we tend to just put in a lot of energy at first and then not sustain it, making too much effort without sustaining power. So we are using the length of an inhalation and the length of an exhalation in order to limit the effort to just this length of time within which to sustain attention. Put forth effort at the beginning of the exhalation to sustain it through that, through the exhalation to the end, and then again with the inhalation. Eventually it becomes even, and one is said to have 'samādhi' when it seems effortless.

At first it seems like a lot of effort, or that we can't do it, because we aren't used to doing this. Most minds have been trained to use

*Ānāpānasati: literally, 'mindfulness' (sati) of the in and out breath.

23

associative thought. The mind has been trained by reading books and the like, to go from one word to the next, to have thoughts and concepts based on logic and reason. However, ānāpānasati is a different kind of training, where the object that we're concentrating on is so simple that it's not at all interesting on the intellectual level. So it's not a matter of being interested in it, but of putting forth effort and using this natural function of the body as a point of concentration. The body breathes whether one is aware of it or not. It's not like pranayama, where we're developing power through the breath, but rather developing samādhi – concentration – and mindfulness through observing the breath, the normal breath, as it is right now. As with anything, this is something that we have to practise to be able to do; nobody has any problem understanding the theory, it's in the continuous practice of it that people feel discouraged.

But note that very discouragement that comes from not being able to get the result that you want, because *that's* the hindrance to the practice. Note that very feeling, recognise that, and then let it go. Go back to the breath again. Be aware of that point where you get fed up or feel aversion or impatience with it, recognise it, then let it go and go back to the breath again.

The Mantra 'Buddho'

If you've got a really active thinking mind, you may find the mantra* 'Buddho' helpful. Inhale on 'Bud' and exhale on '-dho' so you're actually thinking this for each inhalation. This is a way of sustaining concentration: so for the next fifteen minutes, do the ānāpānasati, putting all your attention, composing your mind with the mantric sound, 'Bud-dho'. Learn to train the mind to that point of clarity and brightness rather than just sinking into passivity. It requires sustained effort: one inhalation of 'Bud' – fully bright and clear in your mind, the thought itself raised and bright from the beginning to the end of the inhalation, and '-dho' on the exhalation. Let everything else go at this time. The occasion has arisen now to do just this – you can solve your problems and the world's problems afterwards. At this time this much is all the occasion calls for. Bring the mantra up into consciousness. Make the mantra fully conscious instead of just a perfunctory passive thing that makes the mind dull; energise the mind so that the inhalation on 'Bud' is a bright inhalation, not just a perfunctory 'Bud' sound that fades out because it never gets brightened or refreshed by your mind. You can visualize the spelling so that you're fully with that syllable for the length of an inhalation, from the beginning to the end. Then '-dho' on the exhalation is performed the same way so that there's a continuity of effort rather than sporadic leaps-and-starts and failures.

Just notice if you have any obsessive thoughts that are coming up – some silly phrase that might be going through your mind. Now if you just sink into a passive state, then obsessive thoughts

*mantra: a word of religious significance, the repetition of which is a meditation device.

will take over. But learning to understand how the mind works and how to use it skilfully, you're taking this particular thought, the concept of 'Buddho' (the Buddha, the One Who Knows), and you're holding it in the mind as a thought. Not just as an obsessive, habitual thought, but as a skilful use of thought, using it to sustain concentration for the length of one inhalation, exhalation, for fifteen minutes.

The practice is that, no matter how many times you fail and your mind starts wandering, you simply note that you're distracted, or that you're thinking about it, or you'd rather not bother with 'Buddho' – "I don't want to do that. I'd rather just sit here and relax and not have to put forth any effort. Don't feel like doing it." Or maybe you've got other things on your mind at this time, creeping in at the edges of consciousness – so you note that. Note what mood there is in your mind right now – not to be critical or discouraged, but just calmly, coolly notice, if you're calmed by it, or if you feel dull or sleepy; if you've been thinking all this time or if you've been concentrating. Just to know.

The obstacle to concentration practice is aversion to failure and the incredible desire to succeed. Practice is not a matter of will-power, but of wisdom, of noting wisdom. With this practice, you can learn where your weaknesses are, where you tend to get lost. You witness the kind of character traits you've developed in your life so far, not to be critical of them but just to know how to work with them and not be enslaved by them. This means a careful, wise reflection on the way things are. So rather than avoiding them at all costs, even the ugliest messes are observed and recognised. That's an enduring quality. Nibbāna* is often described as being 'cool'. Sounds like hip talk, doesn't it? But there's a certain significance to that word. Coolness to what? It tends to be refreshing, not caught up in passions but detached, alert and balanced.

---

*Nibbāna: Peace through non-attachment, otherwise spelt 'Nirvāṇa'.

The word 'Buddho' is a word that you can develop in your life as something to fill the mind with rather than with worries and all kinds of unskilful habits. Take the word, look at it, listen to it: 'Buddho'! It means the one who knows, the Buddha, the awakened, that which is awake. You can visualise it in your mind. Listen to what your mind says – blah, blah, blah, etc. It goes on like this, an endless kind of excrement of repressed fears and aversions. So, now, we are recognising that. We're not using 'Buddho' as a club to annihilate or repress things, but as a skilful means. We can use the finest tools for killing and for harming others, can't we? You can take the most beautiful Buddha rupa and bash somebody over the head with it if you want! That's not what we call 'Buddhanussati', Reflection on the Buddha, is it? But we might do that with the word 'Buddho' as a way of suppressing those thoughts or feelings. That's an unskilful use of it. Remember we're not here to annihilate but to allow things to fade out. This is a gentle practice of patiently imposing 'Buddho' over the thinking, not out of exasperation, but in a firm and deliberate way.

The world needs to learn how to do this, doesn't it? – the U.S. and the Soviet Union – rather than taking machine guns and nuclear weapons and annihilating things that get in the way; or saying awful nasty things to each other. Even in our lives we do that, don't we? How many of you have said nasty things to someone else recently, wounding things, unkind barbed criticism, just because they annoy you, get in your way, or frighten you? So we practise just this with the little nasty annoying things in our own mind, the things which are foolish and stupid. We use 'Buddho', not as a club but as a skilful means of allowing it to go, to let go of it. Now for the next fifteen minutes, go back to your noses, with the mantra 'Buddho'. See how to use it and work with it.

Effort and Relaxation

Effort is simply doing what you have to do. It varies according to people's characters and habits. Some people have a lot of energy – so much so that they are always on the go, looking for things to do. You see them trying to find things to do all the time, putting everything into the external. In meditation, we're not seeking anything to do, as an escape, but we are developing the internal kind of effort. We observe the mind, and concentrate on the subject.

If you make too much effort, you just become restless and if you don't put enough effort in, you become dull and the body begins to slump. Your body is a good measure of effort: you make the body straight, you can fill the body with effort; align the body, pull up your chest, keep your spine straight. It takes a lot of will-power so your body is a good thing to watch for effort. If you're slack you just find the easiest posture – the force of gravity pulls you down. When the weather is cold, you have to put energy up through the spine so that you're filling your body out, rather than huddling under blankets.

With ānāpānasati, 'mindfulness of breathing', you are concentrating on the rhythm. I found it most helpful for learning to slow down rather than doing everything quickly – like thinking – you're concentrating on a rhythm that is much slower than your thoughts. But ānāpānasati requires you to slow down, it has a gentle rhythm to it. So we stop thinking: we are content with one inhalation, one exhalation – taking all the time in the world, just to be with one inhalation, from the beginning to the middle and end.

If you're trying to get samādhi (concentration) from ānāpānasati, then you have already set a goal for yourself – you're doing this in order to get something for yourself, so ānāpānasati be-comes a very frustrating experience, you become angry with it. Can you stay with just one inhalation? To be content with just one exhalation? To be content with just the simple little span you have to slow down, don't you?

When you're aiming to get jhāna (absorption) from this medita-tion and you're really putting a lot of effort into it, you are not slowing down, you're trying to get something out of it, trying to achieve and attain rather than humbly being content with one breath. The success of ānāpānasati is just that much – mindful for the length of one inhalation, for the length of one exhalation. Establish your attention at the beginning and the end – or begin-ning, middle and end. This gives you some definite points for reflection, so that if your mind wanders a lot during the practice, you pay special attention, scrutinising the beginning, the middle and the end. If you don't do this, then the mind will tend to wander.

All our effort goes into just that; everything else is suppressed during that time, or discarded. Reflect on the difference between inhalation and exhalation – examine it. Which do you like best? Sometimes the breathing will seem to disappear; it becomes very fine. The body seems to be breathing by itself and you get this strange feeling that you're not going to breathe. It's a bit frightening.

But this is an exercise; you centre on the breathing, without trying to control it at all. Sometimes when you are concentrating on the nostrils, you feel that the whole body is breathing. The body keeps breathing, all on its own.

Sometimes we get too serious about everything – totally lacking in joy and happiness, no sense of humour; we just repress every-thing. So gladden the mind, be relaxed and at ease, taking all the time in the world, without the pressure of having to achieve anything important: nothing special, nothing to attain, no big deal. It's just a little thing; even when you have only one mindful inhalation during the morning, that is better than what most people are doing – surely it is better than being heedless the whole time.

If you're a really negative person then try to be someone who is kinder and more self-accepting. Just relax and don't make meditation into a burdensome task for yourself. See it as an opportunity to be peaceful and at ease with the moment. Relax your body and be at peace.

You're not battling with the forces of evil. If you feel averse towards ānāpānasati, then note that, too. Don't feel that it is something you *have* to do, but see it as a pleasure, as something you really enjoy doing. You don't have to do anything else, you can just be completely relaxed. You've got all you need, you've got your breathing, you just have to sit here, there is nothing difficult to do, you need no special abilities, you don't even need to be particularly intelligent. When you think, "I can't do it," then just recognise that as resistance, fear or frustration and then relax.

If you find yourself getting all tense and up-tight about ānāpānasati, then stop doing it. Don't make it into a difficult thing, don't make it into a burdensome task. If you can't do it, then just sit. When I used to get in terrible states, then I would just contemplate 'peace'. I would start to think, "I've got to... I've got to... I've got to do this." Then I'd think, "Just be at peace, relax."

Doubts and restlessness, discontent, aversion – soon I was able to reflect on peace, saying the word over and over, hypnotising myself, "Relax, relax." The self doubts would start coming, "I'm getting nowhere with this, it's useless, I want to get something." Soon I was able to be peaceful with that. You can calm down and when you relax, you can do ānāpānasati. If you want something to do, then do that.

At first, the practice can get very boring; you feel hopelessly clumsy like when you are learning to play the guitar. When you first start playing, your fingers are so clumsy, it seems hopeless, but once you have done so for some time, you gain skill and it's quite easy. You're learning to witness to what is going on in your mind, so you can know when you're getting restless and tense, averse to everything you recognise that, you're not trying to convince yourself that it is otherwise. You're fully aware of the way things are: what do you do when you're up-tight, tense and nervous? You relax.

In my first years with Ajahn Chah, I used to be very serious about meditation sometimes, I really got much too grim and solemn about myself. I would lose all sense of humour and just get DEAD SERIOUS, all dried up like an old twig. I would put forth a lot of effort, but it would be so strung up and unpleasant, thinking, "I've got to...I'm too lazy." I felt such terrible guilt if I wasn't meditating all the time – a grim, joyless state of mind. So I watched that, meditating on myself as a dried stick. When the whole thing was totally unpleasant, I would just remember the opposites, "You don't have to do anything. Nowhere to go, nothing to do. Be peaceful with the way things are now, relax, let go." I'd use that.

When your mind gets into this condition, apply the opposite, learn to take things easy. You read books about not putting any effort into things – "just let it happen in a natural way" – and you think, "All I have to do is lounge about." Then you usually lapse into a dull, passive state. But that is the time when you need to put forth a bit more effort.

With ānāpānasati, you can sustain effort for one inhalation. And if you can't sustain it for one inhalation, then do it for half an inhalation at least. In this way, you're not trying to become perfect all at once. You don't have to do everything just right, because of some idea of how it could be, but you work with the kind of problems as they are. But if you have a scattered mind, then it is wisdom to recognise the mind that goes all over the place – that's insight. To think that you shouldn't be that way, to hate yourself or feel discouraged because that is the way you happen to be – that's ignorance.

With ānāpānasati, you recognise the way it is now and you start from there: you sustain your attention a little longer and you begin to understand what concentration is, making resolutions that you can keep. Don't make Superman resolutions when you're not Superman. Do ānāpānasati, for ten or fifteen minutes rather than thinking you can do it the whole night, "I'm going to do ānāpānasati from now until dawn." Then you fail and become angry. You set periods that you know you can do. Experiment, work with the mind until you understand how to put forth effort, how to relax.

Ānāpānasati is something immediate. It takes you to insight – vipassanā. The impermanent nature of the breath is not yours, is it? Having been born, the body breathes all on its own. In and out breaths – the one conditions the other. As long as the body is alive, that is the way it will be. You don't control anything, breathing belongs to nature, it doesn't belong to you, it is not-self. When you observe this, you are doing vipassanā, insight. It's not something exciting or fascinating or unpleasant. It's natural.

Walking Mindfully (Jongrom)

Walking 'Jongrom'* is a practice of concentrated walking whereby you're with the movement of your feet. You bring your attention to the walking of the body from the beginning of the path to the end, turning around, and the body standing. Then there arises the intention to walk, and then the walking. Note the middle of the path and the end, stopping, turning, standing: the points for composing the mind when the mind starts wandering everywhichway. You can plan a revolution or something while walking jongrom if you're not careful! How many revolutions have been plotted during jongrom walking...? So, rather than doing things like that, we use this time to concentrate on what's actually going on. These aren't fantastic sensations, they're so ordinary that we don't really notice them. Now notice that it takes an effort to really be aware of things like that.

Now when the mind wanders and you find yourself off in India while you're in the middle of the jongrom path, then recognise – "Oh!" You're awakened at that moment. You're awake, so then re-establish your mind on what's actually happening, with the body walking from this place to that. It's a training in patience because the mind wanders all over the place. If in the past you've had blissful moments of walking meditation and you think, "On the last retreat I did walking jongrom and I really felt just the body walking. I felt that there was no self and it was blissful, oh, if I can't do that again..." Note that desire to attain something according to a memory of some previous happy time. Note that as a condition; that's an obstacle. Give it all up, it doesn't matter whether a moment of bliss comes out of it. Just one step and the next step –

*Jongrom (a Thai word): pacing to and fro on a straight path. *See page 10.*

33

that's all there is to it, a letting go, a being content with very little, rather than trying to attain some blissful state that you might have had at some time while doing this meditation. The more you try, the more miserable your mind becomes, because you're following the desire to have some lovely experience according to a memory. Be content with the way it is now, whatever it is. Be peaceful with the way it is at this moment, rather than rushing around trying to do something now to get some state that you want.

One step at a time – notice how peaceful walking meditation is when all you have to do is be with one step. But if you think you've got to develop samādhi from this walking practice, and your mind goes all over the place, what happens? "I can't stand this walking meditation, get no peace out of it, I've been practising trying get this feeling of walking without anybody walking and my mind just wanders everywhere" – because you don't understand how to do it yet, your mind is idealizing, trying to *get* something, rather than just *being*. When you're walking, all you have to do is walk. One step, next step – simple… But it is not easy, is it? The mind is carried away, trying to figure out what you should be doing, what's wrong with you and why you can't do it.

But in the monastery what we do is to get up in the morning, do the chanting, meditate, sit, clean the monastery, do the cooking, sit, stand, walk, work; whatever, just take it as it comes, one thing at a time. So, being with the way things are is non-attachment, that brings peacefulness and ease. Life changes and we can watch it change, we can adapt to the changingness of the sensory world, whatever it is. Whether it's pleasant or unpleasant, we can always endure and cope with life, no matter what happens to us. If we realise the truth, we realise inner peacefulness.

Kindness (Mettā)

In English the word 'love' often refers to 'something that I like'. For example, "I love sticky rice," "I love sweet mango." We really mean we like it. Liking is being attached to something such as food which we really like or enjoy eating. We don't love it. Mettā means you love your enemy; it doesn't mean you like your enemy. If somebody wants to kill you and you say, "I like them," that is silly! But we can love them, meaning that we can refrain from unpleasant thoughts and vindictiveness, from any desire to hurt them or annihilate them. Even though you might not like them – they are miserable, wretched people – you can still be kind, generous and charitable towards them. If some drunk came into this room who was foul and disgusting, ugly and diseased, and there was nothing one could be attracted to in him – to say, "I like this man" would be ridiculous. But one could love him, not dwell in aversion, not be caught up in reactions to his unpleasantness. That's what we mean by mettā.

Sometimes there are things one doesn't like about oneself, but mettā means not being caught up in the thoughts we have, the attitudes, the problems, the thoughts and feelings of the mind. So it becomes an immediate practice of being very mindful. To be mindful means to have mettā towards the fear in your mind, or the anger, or the jealousy. Mettā means not creating problems around existing conditions, allowing them to fade away, to cease. For example, when fear comes up in your mind, you can have mettā for the fear – meaning that you don't build up aversion to it, you can just accept its presence and allow it to cease. You can also minimise the fear by recognising that it is the same kind of fear that everyone has, that animals have. It's not my fear, it's not a person's,

35

it's an impersonal fear. We begin to have compassion for other beings when we understand the suffering involved in reacting to fear in our own lives – the pain, the physical pain of being kicked, when somebody kicks you. That kind of pain is exactly the same kind of pain that a dog feels when he's being kicked, so you can have mettā for the pain, meaning a kindness and a patience of not dwelling in aversion. We can work with mettā internally, with all our emotional problems: you think, "I want to get rid of it, it's terrible." That's a lack of mettā for yourself, isn't it? Recognise the desire-to-get-rid-of! Don't dwell in aversion on existing emotional conditions. You don't have to pretend to feel approval towards your faults. You don't think, "I like my faults." Some people are foolish enough to say, "My faults make me interesting. I'm a fascinating personality because of my weaknesses." Mettā is not conditioning yourself to believe that you like something that you don't like at all, it is just not dwelling in aversion. It's easy to feel mettā towards something you like – pretty little children, good looking people, pleasant mannered people, little puppies, beautiful flowers – we can feel mettā for ourselves when we're feeling good. "I am feeling happy with myself now." When things are going well it's easy to feel kind towards that which is good and pretty and beautiful. At this point we can get lost. Mettā isn't just good wishes, lovely sentiments, high-minded thoughts, it's always very practical.

If you're being very idealistic, and you hate someone, then you feel, "I shouldn't hate anyone. Buddhists should have mettā for all living beings. I should love everybody. If I'm a good Buddhist then I should like everybody." All that comes from impractical idealism. Have mettā for the aversion you feel, for the pettiness of the mind, the jealousy, envy – meaning peacefully co-existing, not creating problems, not making it difficult nor creating problems out of the difficulties that arise in life, within our minds and bodies.

In London, I used to get very upset when travelling on the underground. I used to hate it, those horrible underground stations with ghastly advertising posters and great crowds of people

36

on those dingy, grotty trains which roar along the tunnels. I used to feel a total lack of mettā (patient-kindness). I used to dwell in aversion on it, then I decided to make my practice a patient-kindness meditation while travelling on the London Underground. Then I began to really enjoy it, rather than dwelling in resentment. I began to feel kindly towards the people there. The aversion and the complaining all disappeared – totally.

When you feel aversion towards somebody, you can notice the tendency to start adding to it, "He did this and he did that, and he's this way and he shouldn't be that way." Then when you really like somebody, "He can do this and he can do that. He's good and kind." But if someone says, "That person's really bad!" you feel angry. If you hate somebody and someone else praises him, you also feel angry. You don't want to hear how good your enemy is. When you are full of anger, you can't imagine that someone you hate may have some virtuous qualities; even if they do have some good qualities, you can never remember any of them. You can only remember all the bad things. When you like somebody, even his faults can be endearing – 'harmless little faults'.

So recognise this in your own experience; observe the force of like and dislike. Patient-kindness, mettā, is a very useful and effective instrument for dealing with all the petty trivia which the mind builds up around unpleasant experience. Mettā is also a very useful method for those who have discriminative, very critical minds. They can see only the faults in everything, but they never look at themselves, they only see what's 'out there'.

It is now very common to always be complaining about the weather or the government. Personal arrogance gives rise to these really nasty comments about everything; or you start talking about someone who isn't there, ripping them apart, quite intelligently, and quite objectively. You are so analytical, you know exactly what that person needs, what they should do and what they should not do, and why they're this way and that. Very impressive to have such a sharp, critical mind and know what they ought to do. You are, of course, saying, "Really, I'm much better than they are."

You are not blinding yourself to the faults and flaws in every-thing. You are just peacefully co-existing with them. You are not demanding that it be otherwise. So mettā sometimes needs to overlook what's wrong with yourself and everyone else – it doesn't mean that you don't notice those things, it means that you don't develop problems around them. You stop that kind of indulgence by being kind and patient – peacefully co-existing.

Mindfulness of the Ordinary

Now for the next hour we'll do the walking practice, using the motion of walking as the object of concentration, bringing your attention to the movement of your feet, and the pressure of the feet touching the ground. You can use the mantra 'Buddho' for that also – 'Bud' for the right, '-dho' for the left, using the span of the jöngrom path. See if you can be fully with, fully alert to the sensation of walking from the beginning of the jongrom path to the end. Use an ordinary pace, then you can slow it down or speed it up accordingly. Develop a normal pace, because our meditation moves around the ordinary things rather than the special. We use the ordinary breath, not a special 'breathing practice'; the sitting posture rather than standing on our heads; normal walking rather than running, jogging or walking methodically slowly – just a relaxed pace. We're practising around what's most ordinary, because we take it for granted. But now we're bringing our attention to all the things we've taken for granted and never noticed, such as our own minds and bodies. Even doctors trained in physiology and anatomy are not really *with* their bodies. They sleep with their bodies, they're born with their bodies, they grow old, have to live with them, feed them, exercise them and yet they'll tell you about a liver as if it was on a chart. It's easier to look at a liver on a chart than to be aware of your own liver, isn't it? So we look at the world as if somehow we aren't a part of it and what's most ordinary, what's most common we miss, because we're looking at what's extraordinary.

Television is extraordinary. They can put all kinds of fantastic adventurous romantic things on the television. It's a miraculous thing, so it's easy to concentrate on. You can get mesmerised by the 'telly'. Also, when the body becomes extraordinary, say it becomes very ill, or very painful, or it feels ecstatic or wonderful feelings go through it, we notice that! But just the pressure of the right foot on the ground, just the movement of the breath, just the feeling of your body sitting on the seat when there's not any kind of extreme sensation – those are the things we're awakened to now. We're bringing our attention to the way things are for an ordinary life.

When life becomes extreme, or extraordinary, then we find we can cope with it quite well. Pacifists and conscientious objectors are often asked this famous question, "You don't believe in violence, so what would you do if a maniac was attacking your mother?" That's something that I think most of us have never had to worry about very much! It's not the kind of ordinary daily occurrence in one's life. But if such an extreme situation did arise, I'm sure we would do something that would be appropriate. Even the nuttiest person can be mindful in extreme situations. But in ordinary life when there isn't anything extreme going on, when we're just sitting here, we can be completely nutty, can't we? It says in the Pātimokkha* discipline that we monks shouldn't hit anyone. So then I sit here worrying about what I would do if a maniac attacks my mother. I've created a great moral problem in an ordinary situation, when I'm sitting here and my mother isn't even here. In all these years there hasn't been the slightest threat to my mother's life from maniacs (from California drivers, yes!). Great moral questions we can answer easily in accordance with time and place if, now, we're mindful of *this* time and *this* place.

So we're bringing attention to the ordinariness of our human condition; the breathing of the body; the walking from one end of the jongrom path to the other; and to the feelings of pleasure and pain. As we go on in the retreat, we examine absolutely everything, watch and know everything as it is. This is our practice of vipassanā – to know things as they are, not according to some theory or some assumption we make about them.

*Pātimokkha: the code of 227 rules and observances that govern the conduct of Buddhist monks of the Theravadin tradition.

Listening to Thought

In opening the mind, or 'letting go', we bring attention to one point on just watching, or being the silent witness who is aware of what comes and goes. With this vipassanā (insight) meditation, we're using the three characteristics of anicca (change), dukkha (unsatisfactoriness), anattā (not self) to observe mental and physical phenomena. We're freeing the mind from blindly repressing, so if we become obsessed with any trivial thoughts or fears, or doubts, worries or anger, we don't need to analyse it. We don't have to figure out why we have it, but just make it fully conscious.

If you're really frightened of something, consciously be frightened. Don't just back away from it, but notice that tendency to try to get rid of it. Bring up fully what you're frightened of, think it out quite deliberately, and listen to your thinking. This is not to analyse, but just to take fear to its absurd end, where it becomes so ridiculous you can start laughing at it. Listen to desire, the mad "I want this, I want that, I've got to have, I don't know what I'll do if I don't have this, and I want that..." Sometimes the mind can just scream away, "I *want* this!" – and you can listen to that.

I was reading about confrontations, where you scream at each other and that kind of thing, say all the repressed things in your mind; this is a kind of catharsis, but it lacks wise reflection. It lacks the skill of listening to that screaming as a condition, rather than just as a kind of 'letting oneself go', and saying what one really thinks. It lacks that steadiness of mind, which is willing to endure the most horrible thoughts. In this way, we're not believing that those are personal problems, but instead taking fear and anger, mentally, to an absurd position, to where they're just seen as a natural progression of thoughts. We're deliberately thinking all the things we're afraid of thinking, not just out of blindness, but actually watching and listening to them as conditions of the mind, rather than personal failures or problems.

So, in this practice now, we begin to let things go. You don't have to go round looking for particular things, but when things which you feel obsessed with keep arising, bothering you, and you're trying to get rid of them, then bring them up even more. Deliberately think them out and listen, like you're listening to someone talking on the other side of the fence, some gossipy old fish-wife: "We did this, and we did that, and then we did this and then we did that..." and this old lady just goes rambling on! Now, practise just listening to it here as a voice, rather than judging it, saying, "No, no, I hope that's not me, that's not my true nature," or trying to shut her up and saying, "Oh, you old bag, I wish you'd go away!" We all have that, even I have that tendency. It's just a condition of nature, isn't it? It's not a person. So, this nagging tendency in us – "I work so hard, nobody is ever grateful" – is a condition, not a person. Sometimes when you're grumpy, nobody can do anything right – even when they're doing it right, they're doing it wrong! That's another condition of the mind, it's not a person. The grumpiness, the grumpy state of mind is known as a condition: anicca – it changes; dukkha – it is not satisfactory; anattā – it is not a person. There's the fear of what others will think of you if you come in late: you've overslept, you come in, and then you start worrying about what everyone's thinking of you for coming in late – "They think I'm lazy." Worrying about what others think is a condition of the mind. Or we're always here on time, and somebody else comes in late, and we think, "They always come in late, can't they ever be on time!" That also is another condition of the mind.

I'm bringing this up into full consciousness, these trivial things, which you can just push aside because they are trivial, and one doesn't want to be bothered with the trivialities of life; but when we don't bother, then all that gets repressed, so it becomes a problem. We start feeling anxiety, feeling aversion to ourselves or to other people, or depressed; all this comes from refusing to allow conditions, trivialities, or horrible things to become conscious.

Then there is the doubting state of mind, never quite sure what to do: there's fear and doubt, uncertainty and hesitation. Deliberately bring up that state of never being sure, just to be relaxed with that state of where the mind is when you're not grasping hold of any particular thing. "What should I do, should I stay or should I go, should I do this or should I do that, should I do ānāpānasati or should I do vipassanā?" Look at that. Ask yourself questions that can't be answered, like "Who am I?" Notice that empty space before you start thinking it – "who?" – just be alert, just close your eyes, and just before you think "who", just look, the mind's quite empty, isn't it? Then, "Who-am-I?", and then the space after the question mark. That thought comes and goes out of emptiness, doesn't it? When you're just caught in habitual thinking, you can't see the arising of thought, can you? You can't see, you can only catch thought after you realise you've been thinking; so start deliberately thinking, and catch the beginning of a thought, before you actually think it. You take deliberate thoughts like, "Who is the Buddha?" Deliberately think that, so that you see the beginning, the forming of a thought, and the end of it, and the space around it. You're looking at thought and concept in a perspective, rather than . just reacting to them.

Say you're angry with somebody. You think, "That's what he said, he said that and he said this and then he did this and he didn't do that right, and he did that all wrong, he's so selfish ... and then I remember what he did to so-and-so, and then ..." One thing goes on to the next, doesn't it? You're just caught in this one thing going on to the next, motivated by aversion. So rather than just being caught in that whole stream of associated thoughts, concepts, deliberately think: "He is the most selfish person I have ever met." And then the ending, emptiness. "He is a rotten egg, a dirty rat, he did this and then he did that," and you can see, it's really funny, isn't it? When I first went to Wat Pah Pong, I used to have tremendous anger and aversion arise. I'd just feel so frustrated, sometimes because I never knew what was really happening, and I didn't want to have to conform so much as I had to there. I was just fuming. Ajahn Chah would be going on – he could give two hour talks in Lao – and I'd have a terrible pain in the knees. So I'd have those thoughts: "Why don't you ever stop talking? I thought Dhamma was simple, why does he have to take two hours to say something?" I'd become very critical of everybody, and then I started reflecting on this and listening to myself, getting angry, being critical, being nasty, resenting, "I don't want this, I don't want that, I don't like this, I don't see why I have to sit here, I don't want to be bothered with this silly thing, I don't know…", on and on. And I kept thinking, "Is that a very nice person that's saying that? Is that what you want to be like, that thing that's always complaining and criticising, finding fault, is that the kind of person you want to be?" "No! I don't want to be like that."

But I had to make it fully conscious to really see it, rather than believe in it. I felt very righteous within myself, and when you feel righteous, and indignant, and you're feeling that they're wrong, then you can easily believe those kinds of thoughts: "I see no need for this kind of thing, after all, the Buddha said … the Buddha would never have allowed this, the Buddha; I know Buddhism!" Bring it up into conscious form, where you can see it, make it absurd, and then you have a perspective on it and it gets quite amusing. You can see what comedy is about! We take ourselves so seriously, "I'm such an important person, my life is so terribly important, that I must be extremely serious about it at all moments. My problems are *so* important, so terribly important; I have to spend a lot of time with my problems because they're so important." One thinks of oneself somehow as very important, so then think it, deliberately think, "I'm a Very Important Person, my problems are very important and serious." When you're thinking that, it sounds funny, it sounds silly, because really, you realise you're not terribly important – none of us are. And the problems we make out of life are trivial things. Some people can ruin their whole lives by creating endless problems, and taking it all so seriously.

If you think of yourself as an important and serious person, then trivial things or foolish things are things that you don't want. If you want to be a good person, and a saintly one, then evil conditions are things that you have to repress out of consciousness. If you want to be a loving and generous type of being, then any type of meanness or jealousy or stinginess is something that you have to repress or annihilate in your mind. So whatever you are most afraid of in your life that you might really be, think it out, watch it. Make confessions: "I want to be a tyrant!", "I want to be a heroin smuggler!" "I want to be a member of the Mafia!", "I want to..." Whatever it is. We're not concerned with the quality of it any more, but the mere characteristic that it's an impermanent condition; it's unsatisfactory, because there's no point in it that can every really satisfy you. It comes and it goes, and it's not self.

The Hindrances and their Cessation

As we listen inwardly, we begin to recognise the whispering voices of guilt, remorse and desire, jealousy and fear, lust and greed. Sometimes you can listen to what lust says: "I want, I've got to have, I've got to have, I want, I want!" Sometimes it doesn't even have any object. You can just feel lust with no object, so you find an object. The desire to get something, "I want something, I want something! I've got to have something, I want..." You can hear that if you listen to your mind. Usually we find an object for lust, such as sex; or we can spend our time fantasizing.

Lust may take the form of looking for something to eat, or anything to absorb into, become something, unite with something. Lust is always on the look-out, always seeking for something. It can be an attractive object which is allowable for monks, like a nice robe or an alms bowl or some delicious food. You can see the inclination to want it, to touch it, to try and somehow get it, own it, possess it, make it mine, consume. And that's lust, that's a force in nature which we must recognise; not to condemn it and say, "I'm a terrible person because I have lust!" – because that's another ego reinforcement, isn't it? As if we are not supposed to have any lust, as if there were any human being who didn't experience desire for something!

These are conditions in nature which we must recognise and see; not through condemnation, but through understanding them. So we get to really know the movement in our mind of lust, greed, seeking something – and the desire-to-get-rid-of. You can witness that also – wanting to get rid of something you have, or some situation, or pain itself. "I want to get rid of the pain I have, I want to get rid of my weakness, I want to get rid of dullness, I want to get rid of my restlessness, my lust. I want to get rid of everything that annoys me. Why did God create mosquitoes? I want to get rid of the pests."

Sensual desire is the first of the hindrances (nīvarana). Aversion is the second one; your mind is haunted with not wanting, with petty irritations and resentments, and then you try and annihilate them. So that's an obstacle to your mental vision, that's a hindrance. I'm not saying we should try to get rid of that hindrance – that's aversion – but to know it, to know its force, to understand it as you experience it. Then you recognise the desire to get rid of things in yourself, the desire to get rid of things around you, desire not to be here, desire not to be alive, desire to no longer exist. That's why we like to sleep, isn't it? Then we can not exist for a while. In sleep consciousness we don't exist because there isn't that same feeling of being alive anymore. That's annihilation. So some people like to sleep a lot because living is too painful for them, too boring, too unpleasant. We get depressed, full of doubt and despair, and we tend to seek an escape through sleep; trying to annihilate our problems, force them out of consciousness.

The third hindrance is sleepiness, lethargy, dullness, sloth, drowsiness, torpor; we tend to react to this with aversion. But this also can be understood. Dullness can be known – the heaviness of body and mind, slow, dull movement. Witness the aversion to it, the wanting to get rid of it. You observe the feeling of dullness in the body and mind. Even the knowledge of dullness is changing, unsatisfactory, not self (anicca, dukkha, anattā).

Restlessness is the opposite of dullness; this is the fourth hindrance. You're not dull at all, you're not sleepy, but restless, nervous, anxious tense. Again, it may have no specific object. Rather than the feeling of wanting to sleep, restlessness is a more obsessive state. You want to do something, run here...do this...do that...talk, go round, run around. And if you have to sit still for a little while when you're feeling restless, you feel penned in, caged;

all you can think of is jumping, running about, doing something. So you can witness that also, especially when you're contained within a form where you can't just follow restlessness. The robes that bhikkhus wear are not conducive to jumping up into trees and swinging from the branches. We can't act out this leaping tendency of the mind, so we have to watch it.

Doubt is the fifth hindrance. Sometimes our doubts may seem very important, and we like to give them a lot of attention. We are very deluded by the quality of it, because it appears to be so substantial: "Some doubts are trivial, yes, but this is an Important Doubt. I've got to know the answer. I've got to be sure. I've got to know definitely, should I do this or should I do that! Am I doing this right? Should I go there, or should I stay here a bit longer? Am I wasting my time? Have I been wasting my life? Is Buddhism the right way or isn't it? Maybe it's not the right religion!" This is doubt. You can spend the rest of your life worrying about whether you should do this or that, but one thing you can know is that doubt is a condition of the mind. Sometimes that tends to be very subtle and deluding. In our position as 'the one who knows', we know doubt is doubt. Whether it's an important or trivial one, it's just doubt, that's all. "Should I stay here, or should I go somewhere else?" It's doubt. "Should I wash my clothes today or tomorrow?" That's doubt. Not very important, but then there are the important ones. "Have I attained Stream Entry yet? What is a Stream Enterer, anyway? Is Ajahn Sumedho an Arahant (enlightened one)? Are there any Arahants at the present time?" Then people from other religions come and say, "Yours is wrong, ours is right!" Then you think, "Maybe they're right! Maybe ours is wrong." What we *can* know is that there is doubt. This is being the knowing, knowing what we can know, knowing that we don't know. Even when you're ignorant of something, if you're aware of the fact that you don't know, then that awareness is knowledge.

So this is being the knowing, knowing what we can know. The Five Hindrances are your teachers, because they're not the inspiring, radiant gurus from the picture books. They can be pretty trivial, petty, foolish, annoying and obsessive. They keep pushing, jabbing, knocking us down all the time until we give them proper attention and understanding, until they are no longer problems. That's why one has to be very patient; we have to have all the patience in the world, and the humility to learn from these five teachers.

And what do we learn? That these are just conditions in the mind; they arise and pass away; they're unsatisfactory, not self. Sometimes one has very important messages in one's life. We tend to believe those messages, but what we *can* know is that those are changing conditions: and if we patiently endure through that, then things change automatically, on their own, and we have the openness and clarity of mind to act spontaneously, rather than react to conditions. With bare attention, with mindfulness, things go on their own, you don't have to get rid of them because everything that begins, ends. There is nothing to get rid of, you just have to be patient with them and allow things to take their natural course into cessation.

When you are patient, allowing things to cease, then you begin to know cessation – silence, emptiness, clarity – the mind clears, stillness. The mind is still vibrant, it's not oblivious, repressed or asleep, and you can hear the silence of the mind.

To allow cessation means that we have to be very kind, very gentle and patient, humble, not taking sides with anything, the good, the bad, the pleasure, or the pain. Gentle recognition allows things to change according to their nature, without interfering. So then we learn to turn away from seeking absorption into the objects of the senses. We find our peace in the emptiness of the mind, in its clarity, in its silence.

Emptiness and Form

When your mind is quiet, listen, and you can hear that vibrational sound in the mind – 'the sound of silence'. What is it? Is it an ear sound, or is it an outward sound? Is it the sound of the mind or the sound of the nervous system, or what? Whatever it is, it's always there, and it can be used in meditation as something to turn toward.

Recognising that all that arises passes away, we begin to look at that which doesn't arise or pass, and is always there. If you start trying to think about that sound, have a name for it, or claim any kind of attainments from it, then of course you are using it in the wrong way. It's merely a standard to refer to when you've reached the limit of the mind, and the end of the mind as far as we can observe it. So from that position you can begin to watch. You can think and still hear that sound (if you're thinking deliberately, that is), but once you're lost in thought, then you forget it and you don't hear it anymore. So if you get lost in thought, then once you're aware that you're thinking again, turn to that sound, and listen to it for a long time. Where before you'd get carried away by emotions or obsessions or the hindrances that arise, now you can practise by gently, very patiently reflecting on the particular condition of the mind as anicca, dukkha, anattā, and then letting go of it. It's a gentle, subtle letting go, not a slam-bang rejection of any condition. So the attitude, the right understanding is more important than anything else. Don't make anything out of that sound of silence. People get excited, thinking they've attained something, or discovered something, but that in itself is another condition you create around the silence. This is a very cool practice, not an exciting one; use it skilfully and gently for letting go, rather than for holding onto a view that you've attained something! If there's anything that blocks anyone in their meditation, it's the view that they've attained something from it!

Now, you can reflect on the conditions of the body and mind and concentrate on them. You can sweep through the body and recognise sensations, such as the vibrations in the hands or feet, or you can concentrate on any point in your body. Feel the sensation of the tongue in the mouth, touching the palate, or the upper lip on top of the lower, or just bring into the consciousness the sensation of wetness of the mouth, or the pressure of the clothes on your body – just those subtle sensations that we don't bother to notice. Reflecting on these subtle physical sensations, concentrate on them and your body will relax. The human body likes to be noticed. It appreciates being concentrated on in a gentle and peaceful way, but if you're inconsiderate and hate the body, it really starts becoming quite unbearable. Remember we have to live within this structure for the rest of our lives. So you'd better learn how to live in it with a good attitude. You say, "Oh, the body doesn't matter, it's just a disgusting thing, gets old, gets sick and dies. The body doesn't matter, it's the mind that counts." That attitude is quite common amongst Buddhists! But it actually takes patience to concentrate on your body, other than out of vanity. Vanity is a misuse of the human body, but this sweeping awareness is skilful. It's not to enforce a sense of ego, but simply an act of goodwill and consideration for a living body – which is not you anyway.

So your meditation now is on the five khandas* and the emptiness of the mind. Investigate these until you fully understand that all that arises passes away and is not self. Then there's no grasping of anything as being oneself, and you are free from that desire to know yourself as a quality or a substance. This is liberation from birth and death.

*khandas: the five categories through which the Buddha summarised the existential human being, i.e. the body (rūpa), feelings (vedanā), perception (saññā), mental formations (saṅkhārā) and the sense consciousness (viññāṇa). In simple terms, 'the body and mind'.

This path of wisdom is not one of developing concentration to get into a trance state, get high and get away from things. You have to be very honest about intention. Are we meditating to run away from things? Are we trying to get into a state where we can suppress all thoughts? This wisdom practice is a very gentle one of even allowing the most horrible thoughts to appear, and let them go. You have an escape hatch, it's like a safety valve where you can let off the steam when there's too much pressure. Normally, if you dream a lot, then you can let off steam in sleep. But no wisdom comes from that, does it? That is just like being a dumb animal; you develop a habit of doing something and then getting exhausted, then crashing out, then getting up, doing something and crashing out again. But this path is a thorough investigation and an understanding of the limitations of the mortal condition of the body and mind. Now you're developing the ability to turn away from the conditioned and to release your identity from mortality.

You're breaking through that illusion that you're a mortal thing – but I'm not telling you that you're an immortal creature either, because you'll start grasping at *that!* "My true nature is one with the ultimate, absolute Truth. I am one with the Lord. My real nature is the Deathless, timeless eternity of bliss." But you notice that the Buddha refrained from using poetic inspiring phrases; not that they're wrong, but because we attach to them. We would settle for that identity with the ultimate, or one with God, or the eternal bliss of the Deathless Realm, and so forth. You get very starry-eyed saying things like that. But it's much more skilful to watch that tendency to want to name or conceive what is inconceivable, to be able to tell somebody else, or describe it just to feel that you have attained something. It is more important to watch that than to follow it. Not that you haven't realised anything, either, but be that careful and that vigilant not to attach to that realisation, because if you do, of course this will just take you to despair again.

If you do get carried away, as soon as you realise you got carried away, then stop. Certainly don't go round feeling guilty about it or being discouraged, but just stop that. Calm down, let go, let go of it. You notice that religious people have insights, and they get very glassy-eyed. Born-again Christians are just aglow with this fervour. Very impressive, too! I must admit, it's very impressive to see people so radiant. But in Buddhism, that state is called 'saññā-vipallāsa'–'meditation madness'. When a good teacher sees you're in that state, he puts you in a hut out in the woods and tells you not to go near anyone! I remember I went like that in Nong Khai the first year before I went to Ajahn Chah, I thought I was fully enlightened, just sitting there in my hut. I knew everything in the world, understood everything. I was just so radiant, and ... but I didn't have anyone to talk to. I couldn't speak Thai, so I couldn't go and hassle the Thai monks. But the British Consul from Vientiane happened to come over one day, and somebody brought him to my hut...and I really let him have it, double barrelled! He sat there in a stunned state, and, being English, he was very, very, very polite, and every time he got up to go I wouldn't let him. I couldn't stop, it was like Niagara Falls, this enormous power coming out, and there was no way I could stop it myself. Finally he left, made an escape somehow: I never saw him again, I wonder why?!

So when we go through that kind of experience, it's important to recognise it. It's nothing dangerous if you know what it is. Be patient with it, don't believe it or indulge in it. You notice Buddhist monks never go around saying much about what 'level of enlightenment' they have – it's just not to be related. When people ask us to teach, we don't teach about our enlightenment, but about the Four Noble Truths as the way for *them* to be enlightened. Nowadays there are all kinds of people claiming to be enlightened or Maitreya Buddhas, avatārs, and all have large followings; people are willing to believe that quite easily! But this particular emphasis of the Buddha is on recognising the way things *are* rather than *believing* in what other people tell us, or say. This is a path of wisdom, in which we're exploring or investigating the limits of the mind. Witness and see: 'sabbe saṅkhārā aniccā', 'all conditioned phenomena are impermanent'; 'sabbe dhammā anattā', 'all things are not self.'

Inner Vigilance

Now, as to the practice of mindfulness. Concentration is where you put your attention on an object, sustain your attention on that one point (such as the tranquillising rhythm of normal breathing), until you become that sign itself, and the sense of subject and object diminishes. Mindfulness, with vipassanā meditation, is the opening of the mind. You no longer concentrate on just one point, but you observe insightfully and reflect on the conditions that come and go, and on the silence of the empty mind. To do this involves letting go of an object; you're not holding on to any particular object, but observing that whatever arises passes away. This is insight meditation, or 'vipassanā'.

With what I call 'inner listening', you can hear the noises that go on in the mind, the desire, the fears, things that you've repressed and have never allowed to be fully conscious. But now, even if there are obsessive thoughts or fears, emotions coming up, then be willing to allow them to become conscious so that you can let them go to cessation. If there's nothing coming or going, then just be in the emptiness, in the silence of the mind. You can hear a high frequency sound in the mind, that's always there, it's not an ear sound. You can turn to that, when you let go of the conditions of the mind. But be honest with your intentions. So if you're turning to the silence, the silent sound of the mind, out of aversion to the conditions, it's just a repression again, it's not purification.

If your intention is wrong, even though you do concentrate on emptiness, you will not get a good result, because you've been misled. You haven't wisely reflected on things, you haven't let anything go, you're just turning away out of aversion, just saying, "I don't want to see that," so you turn away. Now this practice is a patient one of being willing to endure what seems unendurable. It's an inner vigilance, watching, listening, even experimenting. In this practice, the right understanding is the important thing, rather than the emptiness or form or anything like that. Right understanding comes through the reflection that whatever arises, passes away; reflection that even emptiness is not self. If you claim that you are one who's realised emptiness as if you'd attained something, that in itself is wrong intention, isn't it? Thinking you're somebody who has attained or realised on the personal level comes from a sense of self. So we make no claims. If there is something inside you that wants to claim something, then you observe *that* as a condition of the mind.

The sound of silence is always there so you can use it as a guide rather than an end in itself. So it's a very skilful practice of watching and listening, rather than just repressing conditions out of aversion to them. But then the emptiness is pretty boring actually. We're used to having more entertainment. How long can you sit all day being aware of an empty mind, anyway? So recognise that our practice is not to attach to peacefulness or silence or emptiness as an end, but to use it as a skilful means to be the knowing and to be alert. When the mind's empty you can watch – there's still awareness, but you're not seeking rebirth in any condition, because there's not a sense of self in it. Self always comes with the seeking of something or trying to get rid of something. Listen to the self saying, "I want to attain samādhi," "I've got to attain jhāna." That's self talking: "I've got to get first jhāna, second jhāna, before I can do anything," that idea, you've got to get something first. What can you know when you read the teachings from different teachers? You can know when you're confused, when you're doubting, when you're feeling aversion and suspicion. You can know that you're being the knowing, rather than deciding which teacher is the right one.

The mettā practice means to use a gentle kindness by being able to endure what you might believe is unendurable. If you have an obsessed mind that goes on and chats away and nags, and then you want to get rid of it, the more you try to suppress and get rid of it, the worse it gets. And then sometimes it stops and you think, "Oh, I've got rid of it, it's gone." Then it'll start again and you think, "Oh no! I thought I'd got rid of that." So no matter how many times it comes back and goes, or whatever, take it as it comes. Be one who takes one step at a time. When you're willing to be one who has all the patience in the world to be with the existing condition, you can let it cease. The results of allowing things to cease are that you begin to experience release, because you realise that you're not carrying things around that you used to. Somehow things that used to make you angry no longer really bother you very much, and that surprises you. You begin to feel at ease in situations that you never felt at ease in before, because you're allowing things to cease, rather than just holding on and recreating fears and anxieties. Even 'dis-ease' of those around you doesn't influence you. You're not reacting to other's lack of ease by getting tense yourself. That comes through letting go and allowing things to cease.

So the general picture now is for you to have this inner vigilance, and to note any obsessive things that come up. If they keep coming back all the time, then you're obviously attached in some way – either through aversion or infatuation. So, you can begin to recognise attachment rather than just try to get rid of it. Once you can understand it and you can let go, then you can turn to the silence of the mind because there's no point in doing anything else. There's no point in holding on or hanging on to conditions any longer than necessary. Let them cease. When we react to what arises, we create a cycle of habits. A habit is something that is cyclical, it keeps going in a cycle, it has no way of ceasing. But if you let go, and leave things alone, then what arises ceases. It doesn't become a cycle.

So emptiness isn't getting rid of everything; it's not total blankness, but an infinite potential for creation to arise and to pass, without your being deluded by it. The idea of me as a creator, my artistic talents, expressing myself – it's an incredible egotistical trip, isn't it? "This is what I've done, this is mine." They say, "Oh, you're very skilled, aren't you? You're a genius!" Yet so much of creative art tends to be regurgitations of people's fears and desires. It's not really creative; it's just recreating things. It's not coming from an empty mind, but from an ego, which has no real message to give other than that it's full of death and selfishness. On a universal level it has no real message other than "Look at me!" as a person, as an ego. Yet the empty mind has infinite potential for creation. One doesn't think of creating things; but creation can be done with no self and nobody doing it – it happens.

So we leave creation to the Dhamma rather than think that that's something to be responsible for. All we have to do now, all that's necessary for us – conventionally speaking, as human beings, as people – is to let go; or not attach. Let things go. Do good, refrain from doing evil, be mindful. Quite a basic message.

Reflection

The Need for Wisdom in the World

We are here with one common interest among all of us. Instead of a room of individuals all following their own views and opinions, tonight we are all here because of a common interest in the practice of the Dhamma. When this many people come together on Sunday night, you begin to see the potential for human existence, a society based on this common interest in the truth. In the Dhamma we merge. What arises passes, and in its passing is peace. So when we begin to let go of our habits and attachments to the conditioned phenomena, we begin to realise the wholeness and oneness of the mind.

This is a very important reflection for this time, when there are so many quarrels and wars going on because people cannot agree on anything. The Chinese against the Russians, the Americans against the Soviets, and on it goes. Over what? What are they fighting about? About their perceptions of the world. "This is *my* land and I want it *this* way. I want *this* kind of government, and *this* kind of political and economic system," and it goes on and on. It goes on to the point where we slaughter and torture until we destroy the land we are trying to liberate, and enslave or confuse all the people we are trying to free. Why? Because of not understanding the way things are.

The way of the Dhamma is one of observing nature and harmonising our lives with the natural forces. In European civilisation we never really looked at the world in that way. We have idealised it. If everything were an ideal, then it should be a certain way. And when we just attach to ideals, we end up doing what we have done to our earth at this time, polluting it, and being at the point of totally destroying it because we do not understand the limitations placed on us by the earth's conditions. So in all things of this nature, we sometimes have to learn the hard way through doing it all wrong and making a total mess. Hopefully it is not an insoluble situation.

Now, in this monastery the monks and nuns are practising the Dhamma with diligence. For the whole month of January we are not even talking, but dedicating our lives and offering the blessings of our practice for the welfare of all sentient beings. This whole month is a continuous prayer and offering from this community for the welfare of all sentient beings. It is a time just for realisation of truth, watching and listening and observing the way things are; a time to refrain from indulging in selfish habits, moods, to give that all up for the welfare of all sentient beings. This is a sign to all people to reflect on this kind of dedication and sacrifice of moving towards truth. It's a pointer towards realising truth in your own life, rather than just living in a perfunctory, habitual way, following the expedient conditions of the moment. It's a reflection for others. To give up immoral, selfish or unkind pursuits for being one who is moving towards impeccability, generosity, morality and compassionate action in the world. If we do not do this then it is a completely hopeless situation. They might as well just blow it all up because if nobody is willing to use their life for anything more than just selfish indulgence, then it is worthless.

This country is a generous and benevolent country, but we just take it for granted and exploit it for what we can get. We do not think about giving anything to it much. We demand a lot, wanting the Government to make everything nice for us, and then we criticise them when they cannot do it. Nowadays you find selfish individuals living their lives on their own terms, without wisely reflecting and living in a way that would be a blessing to the society as a whole. As human beings we can make our lives into great blessings; or we can become a plague on the landscape, taking the Earth's resources for personal gain and getting as much as we can for ourselves, for 'me' and 'mine'.

In the practice of the Dhamma the sense of 'me' and 'mine' starts fading away – the sense of 'me' and 'mine' as this little creature sitting here that has a mouth and has to eat. If I just follow the desires of my body and emotions, then I become a greedy selfish little creature. But when I reflect on the nature of my physical condition and how it can be skilfully used in this lifetime for the welfare of all sentient beings, then this being becomes a blessing. (Not that one thinks of oneself as a blessing, "I am a blessing"; it is another kind of conceit if you start attaching to the idea that you are a blessing!) So one is actually living each day in a way that one's life is something that brings joy, compassion, kindness, or at least is not causing unnecessary confusion and misery. The least we can do is keep the Five Precepts* so that our bodies and speech are not being used for disruption, cruelty and exploitation on this planet. Is that asking too much of any of you? Is it too fantastic to give up just doing what you feel like at the moment in order to be at least a little more careful and responsible for what you do and say? We can all try to help, be generous and kind and considerate to the other beings that we have to share this planet with. We can all wisely investigate and understand the limitations we are under, so that we are no longer deluded by the sensory world. This is why we meditate. For a monk or nun this is a way of life, a sacrifice of our particular desires and whims for the welfare of the community, of the Saṅgha.

If I start thinking of myself and of what I want, then I forget about the rest of you because what I particularly want at the moment might not be good for the rest of you. But when I use this refuge in Saṅgha as my guide, then the welfare of the Saṅgha is my joy and I

*The Five Precepts are the basic moral precepts to be observed by every practising Buddhist.

give up my personal whims for the welfare of the Saṅgha. That is why the monks and nuns all shave their heads and live under the discipline established by the Buddha. This is a way of training oneself to let go of self as a way of living: a way that brings no shame or guilt or fear into one's life. The sense of disruptive individuality is lost because one is no longer determined to be independent from the rest, or to dominate, but to harmonise and live for the welfare of all beings, rather than for the welfare of oneself.

The lay community has the opportunity to participate in this. The monks and nuns are dependent upon the lay community just for basic survival, so it is an important thing for the lay community to take that responsibility. That takes you lay people out of your particular problems and obsessions because when you take time to come here to give, to help, to practise meditation and listen to the Dhamma, we find ourselves merging in that oneness of truth. We can be here together without envy, jealousy, fear, doubt, greed or lust because of our inclination towards realising that truth: Make that the intention for your life; don't waste your life on foolish pursuits!

This truth, it can be called many things. Religions try to convey that truth in some ways – through concepts and doctrines – but we have forgotten what religion is about. In the past hundred years or so, our society has been following materialistic science, rational thought and idealism based on our ability to conceive of political and economic systems, yet we cannot make them work, can we? We cannot really create a democracy or a true communism or a true socialism – we cannot create that because we are still deluded by the sense of self. So it ends up in tyranny and in selfishness, fear and suspicion. So the present world situation is a result of not understanding the way things are, and a time when each one of us, if we really are concerned about what we can do, has to make our own life into something worthy. Now how do we do this?

Firstly, you have to admit the kind of motivations and selfish indulgence of emotional immaturity in order to know them and be able to let them go; to open the mind to the way things are, to be alert. Just our practice of ānapānasati is a beginning, isn't it? It's not just another habit or pastime you develop to keep you busy, but a means of putting forth effort to observe, concentrate and be with the way the breath is. You might instead spend a lot of time watching television, going to the pub and doing all kinds of things that are not very skilful – somehow that seems more important than spending any time watching your own breath, doesn't it? You watch the T.V. news and see people being slaughtered in Lebanon – somehow it seems more important than just sitting watching your inhalation and exhalation. But this is the mind that does not understand the ways things are; so we are willing to watch the shadows on the screen and the misery that can be conveyed through a television screen about greed, hatred and stupidity, carried on in a most despicable way. Wouldn't it be much more skilful to spend that time being with the way the body is right now? It would be better to have respect for this physical being here so that one learns not to exploit it, misuse it, and then resent it when it doesn't give you the happiness that you want.

In the monastic life we don't have television because we dedicate our lives to doing more useful things, like watching our breath and walking up and down the forest path. The neighbours think we are dotty. Every day they see people going out wrapped up in blankets and walking up and down. "What are they doing? They must be crazy!" We had a fox hunt here a couple of weeks ago. The hounds were chasing foxes through our woods (doing something really useful and beneficial for all sentient beings!). Sixty dogs and all these grown up people chasing after a wretched little fox. It would be better to spend the time walking up and down a forest path, wouldn't it? Better for the fox, for the dogs, for Hammer Wood and for the foxhunters. But people in West Sussex think they are normal. *They* are the normal ones and *we* are the nutty ones. When we watch our breath and walk up and down the forest path at least we are not terrorising foxes! How would you feel if sixty dogs were chasing you? Just imagine what your heart would do if you had a pack of sixty dogs chasing after you and people on horseback telling them to get you. It's ugly when you really reflect on this. Yet that is considered normal, or even a desirable thing to do in this part of England. Because people do not take time to reflect, we can be victims of habit, caught in desires and habits. If we really investigated fox hunting, we wouldn't do it. If you have any intelligence and really consider what that is about, you would not want to do it. Whereas with simple things like walking up and down on a forest path, and watching your breath, you begin to be aware and much more sensitive. The truth begins to be revealed to us through just the simple, seemingly insignificant practices that we do. Just as when we keep the Five Precepts that is a field of blessing to the world.

When you start reflecting on the way things are and remember when your life has really been in danger, you will know how horrible it is. It is an absolutely terrifying experience. One doesn't intentionally want to subject any other creature to that experience, if you have reflected on it. There is no way in which one is intentionally going to subject another creature to that terror. If you do not reflect, you think foxes do not matter, or fish do not matter. They are just there for my pleasure – it is something to do on a Sunday afternoon. I can remember one woman who came to see me and was very upset about us buying the Hammer Pond*. She said, "You know I get so much peace; I don't come here to fish, I come here for the peacefulness of being here." She spent every Sunday out catching fish just to be at peace. I thought she looked quite healthy, she was a little plump, she was not starving to death.

*Being part of a Buddhist monastery, Hammer Wood and Pond of course became wildlife sanctuaries.

She did not really need to fish for survival. I said, "Well, you could, if you don't need to fish for survival – you have enough money, I hope, to buy fish – you could come here after we buy this pond, and you could just meditate here. You don't have to fish." She didn't want to meditate! Then she went on about rabbits eating her cabbages, so she had to put out all kinds of things that would kill rabbits to keep them from eating her cabbages. This woman never reflects on *anything*. She is begrudging those rabbits her cabbages, but she can very well go out and buy cabbages. But rabbits *can't*. Rabbits have to do the best they can by eating someone else's cabbages. But she never really opened her mind to the way things are, to what is truly kind and benevolent. I would not say she was a cruel or heartless person, just an ignorant middle class woman who never reflected on nature or realised the way the Dhamma is. So she thinks that cabbages are there for her and not for rabbits, and fish are there so that she can have a peaceful Sunday afternoon torturing them.

Now this ability to reflect and observe is what the Buddha was pointing to in his teachings, as the liberation from the blind following of habit and convention. It is a way to liberate this being from the delusion of the sensory condition through wise reflection on the way things are. We begin to observe ourselves, the desire for something, or the aversion, the dullness or the stupidity of the mind. We are not picking and choosing or trying to create pleasant conditions for personal pleasure, but are even willing to endure unpleasant or miserable conditions in order to understand them as just that, and be able to let them go. We are starting to free ourselves from running away from things we don't like. We also begin to be much more careful about how we do live. Once you see what it is all about, you really want to be very, very careful about what you do and say. You can have no intention to live life at the expense of any other creature. One does not feel that one's life is so much more important than anyone else's. One begins to feel the freedom and the lightness in that harmony with nature rather than the heaviness of exploitation of nature for personal gain. When you open the mind to the truth, then you realise there is nothing to fear. What arises passes away, what is born dies, and is not self – so that our sense of being caught in an identity with this human body fades out. We don't see ourselves as some isolated, alienated entity lost in a mysterious and frightening universe. We don't feel overwhelmed by it, trying to find a little piece of it that we can grasp and feel safe with, because we feel at peace with it. Then we have merged with the truth.

The Refuges and Precepts

The 'Going for Refuge' and taking the Precepts define a person as a practising Buddhist.

Going for Refuge gives a continual perspective on life by referring one's conduct and understanding to the qualities of Buddha (wisdom), Dhamma (truth) and Sangha (virtue). The Precepts are also for reflection and to define one's actions as a responsible human being.

There is a formal means of requesting the Refuges and Precepts from a bhikkhu or nun, which is as follows:

The lay person should bow three times and, with hands in añjali*, recite the following:

MAYAM/AHAM BHANTE *(AYYE)* TI-SARANENA SAHA PAÑCA SĪLĀNI YĀCĀMA/YĀCĀMI
We/I, Venerable Sir *(Sister)*, request the Three Refuges and the Five Precepts

DUTIYAMPI MAYAM/AHAM BHANTE *(AYYE)*...
For the second time we/I...

TATIYAMPI MAYAM/AHAM BHANTE *(AYYE)*...
For the third time we/I...

The bhikkhu or nun will then recite the following three times, after which the lay person should repeat three times:

NAMO TASSA BHAGAVATO ARAHATO SAMMĀSAMBUDDHASSA
Homage to the Blessed One, the Noble One, and Perfectly Enlightened One.

The bhikkhu or nun will then recite the following line by line, which the lay person should repeat line by line:

BUDDHAM SARANAM GACCHĀMI
To the Buddha I go for Refuge.

*Añjali: the hands are held vertically, with palms together, close to the chest.

DHAMMAM SARANAM GACCHĀMI
To the Dhamma I go for Refuge.

SAṄGHAM SARANAM GACCHĀMI
To the Sangha I go for Refuge.

DUTIYAMPI BUDDHAM SARANAM GACCHĀMI
For the second time...

DUTIYAMPI DHAMMAM SARANAM GACCHĀMI
For the second time...

DUTIYAMPI SAṄGHAM SARANAM GACCHĀMI
For the second time...

TATIYAMPI BUDDHAM SARANAM GACCHĀMI
For the third time...

TATIYAMPI DHAMMAM SARANAM GACCHĀMI
For the third time...

TATIYAMPI SAṄGHAM SARANAM GACCHĀMI
For the third time...

The bhikkhu or nun then says:

TISARANA – GAMANAM NITTHITAM
This completes the going to the Three Refuges.

The lay person responds:

ĀMA BHANTE *(AYYE)*
Yes, Venerable Sir *(Sister)*.

The bhikkhu or nun then recites the Precepts singly, and the lay person repeats line by line:

1. PĀNĀTIPĀTĀ VERAMANĪ SIKKHĀPADAM SAMĀDIYĀMI
   I undertake the precept to refrain from destroying living creatures.

2. ADINNĀDĀNĀ VERAMANĪ SIKKHĀPADAM SAMĀDIYĀMI
   I undertake the precept to refrain from taking that which is not given.

3. KĀMESU MICCHĀCĀRĀ VERAMAṆĪ SIKKHĀPADAṀ
   SAMĀDIYĀMI
   I undertake the precept to refrain from sexual misconduct.

4. MUSĀVĀDĀ VERAMAṆĪ SIKKHĀPADAṀ SAMĀDIYĀMI
   I undertake the precept to refrain from incorrect speech.

5. SURĀ-MERAYA-MAJJA-PAMĀDAṬṬHĀNĀ VERAMAṆĪ
   SIKKHĀPADAṀ SAMĀDIYĀMI
   I undertake the precept to refrain from intoxicating liquors
   and drugs which lead to carelessness.

After the Five Precepts have been taken, the bhikkhu or nun will
conclude with the following:

IMĀNI PAÑCA SIKKHĀPADĀNI
These Five Precepts

SĪLENA SUGATIṀ YANTI
Have morality as a vehicle for happiness,

SĪLENA BHOGASAMPADĀ
Have morality as a vehicle for good fortune,

SĪLENA NIBBUTIṀ YANTI
Have morality as a vehicle for liberation.

TASMĀ SĪLAṀ VISODHAYE
Let morality therefore be purified.

After taking the Precepts, the lay person then bows three times to
the bhikkhu or nun.

Pronunciation:

ā	as in f*a*ther	u	as in g*oo*d
a	as in *a*bout	e	as in s*ay*
i	as in h*i*t	c, cc	as in *ch*urch
ī	as in mach*i*ne	ñ	as in ca*ny*on
o	as in fl*o*w	ṁ	as in ha*ng*

73

The Text

The material in this book has been edited from talks given at Chithurst Forest Monastery in January 1984, with the exception of three sections. These are 'Effort and Relaxation', 'Kindness (Mettā)' and 'The Hindrances and Their Cessation', which were taken from talks given at the International Forest Monastery, Ubon, N.E. Thailand in December 1982.

The Photographs

The photographs are of slabs from the ruins of the ancient stupa at Amarāvatī in Andhra Pradesh, India; they are reproduced by kind permission of the Trustees of the British Museum, London.

Investigation (page 12): the stupa, a monumental reliquary, contains the relics of a saint. As the object of pigrimages, it symbolizes the universal quest for spiritual truth.

Instruction (page 22): the iconographical footprints of the Buddha. They represent the path that a teacher has taken, to be followed by his disciples.

Reflection (page 60): the lotus of wisdom in a scene of everyday human activity.